To:

Jake Joseph Choplick

From:

Grandpa Brink & Grandma Bobbie

Date:

July 14, 2013

Growing Up Cowboy

Artwork by
Jack Sorenson

Text by
Hope Lyda

HARVEST HOUSE PUBLISHERS
EUGENE, OREGON

*Live a good, honorable life. Then, when you get older
and think back, you'll enjoy it a second time.*

COWBOY PROVERB

GROWING UP COWBOY

Text copyright © 2008 by Harvest House Publishers
Published by Harvest House Publishers
Eugene, Oregon 97402
www.harvesthousepublishers.com

ISBN-13: 978-0-7369-2228-9
ISBN-10: 0-7369-2228-8

Design and production by Koechel Peterson & Associates, Inc.,
Minneapolis, Minnesota

Artwork © by Jack Sorenson Fine Art, Inc. and may not be reproduced
without permission. For more information regarding artwork featured in
this book, please contact:

Rich Wiseman, LLC
Fine Art and Gift Licensing
7 Avenida Vista Grande #250
Santa Fe, NM 87508
(505) 466-1927

Scripture quotations come from *The Living Bible*, Copyright © 1971. Used
by permission of Tyndale House Publishers, Inc., Wheaton, IL 60189 USA.
All rights reserved.

Printed in China

08 09 10 11 12 13 14 15 16 / LP / 10 9 8 7 6 5 4 3 2 1

Contents

I consider myself very blessed to have grown up cowboy. I was seven when my father bought a branch canyon west of Palo Duro Canyon State Park near Amarillo, Texas. It was once part of the historic JA Ranch, which had been operated by Charles Goodnight. Our canyon is known as Timbercreek, and it was heaven on earth for a boy.

Our family built Six Gun City, an Old West frontier town and tourist attraction. My numerous jobs included gunfighter and stagecoach driver. We operated a dude ranch and a riding stable. I've been horse-crazy all my life. I would spend up to ten hours a day in the saddle when I wasn't in school.

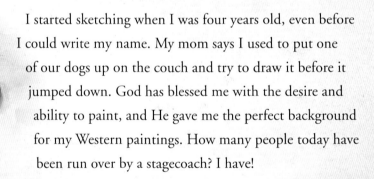

I started sketching when I was four years old, even before I could write my name. My mom says I used to put one of our dogs up on the couch and try to draw it before it jumped down. God has blessed me with the desire and ability to paint, and He gave me the perfect background for my Western paintings. How many people today have been run over by a stagecoach? I have!

My favorite paintings are those that tell a story. The paintings in this book tell the story of my childhood and the wonder of what it's like to grow up cowboy.

ARTIST JACK SORENSON

A New Frontier

Little boys are born with the spirit of the cowboy! They find adventure at every turn, lasso anything that moves (and doesn't move), wrangle the last chicken nugget from their sibling, and charge toward open spaces with fearlessness.

Our hope for them is as wide as a new frontier and our love and prayers for them are as deep as a canyon. As they grow, we want to instill in our boys the characteristics that will help them become men of good character. Today's young cowboy is tomorrow's man of big dreams and a heart of honor. Follow along with your favorite cowpoke as we round up these special traits and virtues and ride toward the promising horizon of a little boy's future.

*There's nothing that can help you understand your beliefs
more than trying to explain them to an inquisitive child.*

FRANK A. CLARK

*When one asked him what boys
should learn, "That," said he,
"which they shall use when men."*

PLUTARCH

*A boy has two jobs.
One is just being a boy.
The other is growing up
to be a man.*

HERBERT HOOVER

A Growing Cowboy Is
Respectful

Boys reach for anything in their line of sight. Through their shiny eyes, the world is full of objects—from books to glasses to dog food—that are theirs for the taking. What a perfect opportunity to teach respect! It's a big concept for a little one, so start with the basics: respecting people and their things. Instead of a constant cry of "Don't touch that!" explain the reason. "Your grandfather likes to have his glasses by his reading chair, so let's do that for him." If your boy is quick to interrupt others, explain the pacing of listening and talking so everyone gets a chance. Developing the art of conversation at an early age will help your boy convey respect, and it will serve him well in the future.

Teach your cowpoke to rein in his quick draw hands and his words. Other characteristics of honor will grow from a boy's desire to respect himself, his family, his friends, his teachers, and those he meets wherever his life trail leads.

Teach a child to choose the right path,
And when he is older he will remain upon it.

The Book of Proverbs

The childhood shows the man
As morning shows the day.

John Milton

A fairly bright boy is far more intelligent and
far better company than the average adult.

John B.S. Haldane

A Growing Cowboy Is
Polite

When a cowboy leaves his home on the range and heads for town, he knows it's important to pack his manners with him. "Pardon me, ma'am," he says when a lady passes by him on the sidewalk. He removes his hat, bows his head, and offers a polite smile.

Little boys can learn the importance of manners with a bit of encouragement and repetition. Dinnertime is a great opportunity to make manners a natural part of daily living. "Please pass the mashed potatoes." "Thank you for the good meal." "Mother, may I be excused from the table?" Now and then he'll need a cue to use his best behavior, but soon your little cowboy will understand that even when he leaves home it's important to have his manners along!

Children are our most valuable natural resource.

HERBERT HOOVER

As soon as a child is able to extend a chubby little hand and ask for a cookie, you should encourage him to say "please." As soon as he is old enough to be given a gift, prompt him to say "thank you." As soon as he can offend another person, "I'm sorry" should become part of his vocabulary. Your child may still believe he's the center of the universe, but his words should reveal a person who cares for others' feelings.

SHERYL EBERLY
365 Manners Kids Should Know

A Growing Cowboy Is
Honest

Has your son ever stood front and center in a group and revealed something embarrassing but true? Bless them…kids are often honest to the point of "too much information." But as they get a bit older, they see how their responses can determine their fate. And the wheels of their quick minds begin to turn. It's easy for big fibs to fall from sweet little lips when it seems the best way out of a predicament. "It wasn't me!"

Model for him how to be honest even when the outcome isn't comfortable. A reliable boy is one who can be depended upon for small and large tasks. As he builds a foundation of trust, honor him with more responsibility and freedom.

I hope I shall always possess firmness and virtue enough to maintain what I consider the most enviable of all titles, the character of an "Honest Man."

GEORGE WASHINGTON

If parents want honest children, they should be honest themselves.

ROBERT G. INGERSOLL

Be in general virtuous, and you will be happy.

BENJAMIN FRANKLIN

Cowboy courage can be witnessed in boys at play. As they wear capes, swing swords, shout directions to imagined allies, and brace themselves for battle with fantasy foes, they are expressing valiant hearts! Encourage your young man to be brave in real life too.

Brave boys get back up after a fall on the playground. Brave boys befriend the kid who is picked on during recess. Brave boys are honest about what they've done. Brave boys keep trying new things, even when their first attempts don't turn out so great. Brave boys stand up for their friends, their beliefs, and their values. Applaud the bold actions and words your son musters today. He'll become a man of cowboy courage who is ready and willing to do the right thing.

Oh, the eagerness and freshness of youth!
How the boy enjoys his food, his sleep,
his sports, his companions, his truant days!
His life is an adventure, he is widening
his outlook, he is extending his dominion,
he is conquering his kingdom.

JOHN BURROUGHS

What a new face courage puts on everything!
RALPH WALDO EMERSON

Courage is resistance to fear, mastery of fear—
not absence of fear.
MARK TWAIN

A Growing Cowboy Is
Joyful

Every little cowboy is born with the ability to discover joy wherever it can be found. Life can be simple, complicated, busy, or slow-paced, and little boys can make the most out of almost any situation. Sometimes adults lose their way and begin to turn toward serious matters or the what-ifs of a predicament, but if they will take the time to listen to the bubbling joy the smallest boy is eager to offer, their lives will be better for it.

To prepare for times when the clouds of trouble approach, teach your boy about more than the silver lining. Inspire your little one to embrace wonder. "That cloud looks a lot like Uncle Jack's moustache. And that one reminds me of an upside-down giraffe." Turn any moment—a trial or celebration—into a lesson about resting in and shaping a life with joy.

You are worried about seeing him spend his early years in doing nothing. What! Is it nothing to be happy? Nothing to skip, play, and run around all day long? Never in his life will he be so busy again.

JEAN-JACQUES ROUSSEAU

Delight and liberty, the simple creed of Childhood, whether busy or at rest.

WILLIAM WORDSWORTH

There are no seven wonders of the world in the eyes of a child. There are seven million.

WALT STREIGHTIFF

A Growing Cowboy Is
Generous

When little ones discover how to grab an object, their next revelation is to grab and go trundling off with the desired item in their clutches as their peals of laughter offer a built-in burglar alarm. "Mine!" they call out to whichever adult is chasing them down. This is a good time in a boy's upbringing to introduce how the opposite action also offers much joy—giving. Releasing a present, an emotion, a good thought, or an idea can be as much fun as the grab-and-go scenario.

Show your cowboy the simplest and most meaningful ways to be generous. Nurture their ability to see what others need. Rarely is it about money or things. Often it is about tenderness, kindness, and compassion. Show your boy a true spirit of generosity, and he'll take it and run with it through the rest of his days.

One of the best things in the world is to be a boy;
It requires no experience, but needs some practice to be a good one.

CHARLES DUDLEY WARNER

A child's eyes! Those clear wells of undefiled thought! What on earth can be more beautiful?
Full of hope, love, and curiosity, they meet your own. In prayer, how earnest!
In joy, how sparkling! In sympathy, how tender!

CAROLINE NORTON

He knows when you're happy
He knows when you're comfortable
He knows when you're confident
And he always knows when you have carrots.

AUTHOR UNKNOWN

A Growing Cowboy Is
Hopeful

It becomes second nature to warn young ones of the dangers that lurk beyond the safe territory of home. We grab for a little boy's hand at the intersection and express concern if strangers are near. But don't forget to embrace the hopefulness of life. Every cowboy had to face the risks of rough mountain rides or uncertainties of what awaited up ahead. But what kept them in their saddles and moving in a forward direction was that strong sense of hope and possibility. Surely they felt it with every sunset and sunrise; and they carried this assurance of hope with them just as they did their other essentials—a hat, sense of direction, and a lasso.

Next time you reach for your little cowboy's hand, take a moment to point to the rainbow above, the curious grasshopper below, or the exciting activity just a day ahead. Point the way to the life of hope that surrounds him.

The grand essentials of happiness are: something to do, something to love, and something to hope for.

ALLAN K. CHALMERS

Hope is the parent of faith.

C. A. BARTOL

To drown out the lonely quiet of his journey, Hank started to sing. It was a cowboy song Mama had learned somewhere:

"Come all you melancholy folks
Wherever you may be,
I'll sing you about the cowboy
Whose life is light and free…"

For a long time he had wanted to be a cowboy. That's what he would do out West.

IRENE BENNETT BROWN
Run from a Scarecrow

When a young cowboy-in-training looks around at his landscape, he sees the chance for adventure. Natural and man-made inventions can present afternoons packed with fun and the thrill of exploration—a tree with limbs positioned for climbing, a tire swing dangling near the local pond, a meandering sidewalk through a new park.

Direct your little one toward his sense of adventure. It might arise when he possesses a fist full of crayons or is given his first basketball. When something delights his senses and he expresses excitement to try something new, lead the way with encouragement, support, and maybe a few stories of the time you made the most enviable pirate ship out of cardboard when you were nine. Together you will discover a new land of wonders.

Boys are found everywhere—on top of, underneath, inside of, climbing on, swinging from, running around, or jumping to. Mothers love them, little girls hate them, older sisters and brothers tolerate them, adults ignore them, and Heaven protects them. A boy is Truth with dirt on its face, Beauty with a cut on its finger, Wisdom with bubble gum in its hair, and the Hope of the future with a frog in its pocket.

ALAN BECK

There comes a time in every rightly constructed boy's life when he has a raging desire to go somewhere and dig for hidden treasure.

MARK TWAIN

My father used to play with my brother and me in the yard. Mother would come out and say, "You're tearing up the grass." "We're not raising grass," Dad would reply. "We're raising boys."

HARMON KILLEBREW

A Growing Cowboy Is
Compassionate

A compassionate heart is planted in a boy when he learns to give selflessly and with love. Provide opportunities for your little guy to give. As a family sponsor a child from another country. Help your son understand that there's a lot of need in the world while modeling that compassion begins at home.

Set up a jar in a kitchen to collect loose change; let him decide where to donate the money. Let your boy lead you in the bedtime prayers. A child's prayers are filled with many innocent requests and often surprising insights into the needs of people around him. Cultivate your son's heart of compassion. The world needs it!

But it so happened that Nature had given to the youngest son gifts which she had not bestowed upon his elder brothers. He had a beautiful face and a fine, strong, graceful figure; he had a bright smile and a sweet, gay voice; he was brave and generous, and had the kindest heart in the world, and seemed to have the power to make every one love him.

FRANCES HODGES BURNETT
Little Lord Fauntleroy

Giving is the secret of a healthy life…not necessarily money, but encouragement, sympathy, and understanding.
JOHN D. ROCKEFELLER

*My horse's feet are as swift as rolling thunder
He carries me away from all my fears
And when the world threatens to fall asunder
His mane is there to wipe away my tears.*

BONNIE LEWIS

A Growing Cowboy Is
Helpful

You know that extra pair of hands you're always asking for? Well, they're right beside you. They might be smudged with peanut butter, but they're available. We tend to newborns with such attentiveness that we sometimes forget that a growing boy is able to do things for himself. Put his energy and ability toward rounding up his clothes for laundry day, making his bed each morning, raking leaves when autumn gives way to winter. Add various age-appropriate tasks as he grows. Teach him that being helpful isn't a "chore" but a way to become a big boy and contribute to the home and the family. Show him ways he can help others—friends, neighbors, family—and he'll grow to be responsible and conscientious.

A helpful boy becomes a man who can care for himself and for others…and who wants to do that very thing.

Childhood is the fiery furnace in which we are melted down
to essentials and that essential shaped for good.
KATHERINE ANNE PORTER

I would be true, for there are those who trust me;
I would be pure, for there are those that care.
I would be strong, for there is much to suffer,
I would be brave, for there is much to dare.
I would be friend to all—the foe, the friendless;
I would be giving, and forget the gift.
I would be humble, for I know my weakness;
I would look up—and laugh—and love—and lift.
HOWARD ARNOLD WALTER, *My Creed*

A Growing Cowboy Is
Full of Dreams

Dreams don't just happen after bedtime prayers are spoken and the night-light glimmers in the evening shadows. They are formed during the waking hours for every little cowboy. When boys gaze off into the distance, they might be looking at the bird on the neighbor's post, but most likely they are imagining what it would be like to be a bird…or a jet pilot! If your little one asks about what you were like as a child, they're also inviting a conversation about the dreams every child holds and about the ones you still have today.

Best of all, dreams are not just for ourselves. We can have great hopes and prayers for the boys in our life, and we can teach them how to express their grand wishes of happiness, healing, success, and joy for others. The next time your little cowboy gazes at an unknown horizon during dinner, beckon his thoughts back to the table, but don't forget to ask for the daydream details—his ideas and hopes are part of what will shape his heart and purpose as a man.

Will thought that roping fence posts was more exciting than history, and swapping ponies was much more fun than math…When he should have been doing chores, he could usually be found in a shady place playing with his rope. He spent most of his after-school time racing his pony with his friends. His parents thought Will should spend more time doing his homework, but Will saw himself as a cowboy in the making.

From WILL ROGERS: *Quotable Cowboy*

There's a long, long trail a-winding
Into the land of my dreams,
Where the nightingales are singing,
And a white moon beams.
There's a long, long night of waiting
Until my dreams all come true,
Till the day when I'll be going down
That long, long trail with you.

STODDARD KING

There is nothing like a dream
to create the future.

VICTOR HUGO

A Growing Cowboy Is
Hardworking

Those who entered the cowboy world were destined for hard work and needed strength and a mighty dose of grit. They faced difficult weather, unknown lands, and the hard job of protecting their herd, and they did it with courage and perseverance. To a cowboy, it was all in a day's work.

Your little cowboy faces daily tasks that seem huge to a young mind or uncoordinated fingers. There might be moments of frustration or even tears, but as you offer advice and the tools he needs, hold back the reins on your desire to do it for him. Boys learn from their mistakes, and they gain confidence in their achievements. Be ready to offer help, but give your cowpoke the space he needs to learn the rewards of hard work and the satisfaction of a job well done. And don't forget to tell him how proud you are of his efforts, no matter the outcome.

Children need models more than they need critics.
JOSEPH JOUBERT

A good scout must be chivalrous. That is, he should be as manly as the knights or pioneers of old. He should be unselfish. He should show courage. He must do his duty. He should show benevolence and thrift. He should be loyal to his country. He should be obedient to his parents, and show respect to those who are his superiors. He should be very courteous to women. One of his obligations is to do a good turn every day to some one.
FROM THE *Boy Scouts Handbook,* 1911

We worry about what a child will become tomorrow, yet we forget that he is someone today.
STACIA TAUSCHER

To a young boy, waiting is a physical exercise. His face will scrunch up in agony at the thought of waiting to go out and play with his friends. He'll double over when snacks are delayed. Despite the extreme responses, practicing patience is one of the best things for your little cowboy. Cultivate a patient nature in your boy with activities that teach him to focus like coloring, reading, and building with blocks. Encourage him to finish tasks he starts and to take pride in a job well done through effort and endurance.

Try to carve out times for quiet in your home to inspire peacefulness and to encourage thoughtful conversations. Go for walks and give him time to examine rocks and count leaves. And soothe his worries when he's waiting for a thunderstorm to pass. Your love and gentleness will show him the way to patience for a lifetime.

The greatest gift we can give one another is rapt attention to one another's existence.
SUE ATCHLEY EBAUGH

*"It is not enough for a man to learn how to ride;
he must learn how to fall."*
MEXICAN PROVERB

*Endurance is the crowning quality,
And patience all the passion of great hearts.*
JAMES RUSSELL LOWELL

Patience is the best remedy for every trouble.
PLAUTUS

A Growing Cowboy Is
Grateful

Your little one will get so much joy out of life if he learns the importance of gratitude. Introduce him to the wonder of all his blessings. Count stars in the night sky from the back porch. Talk about the love of family. At dinner have each person share what they are most thankful for that day. Teach your boy to say "thank you" and to wear an attitude of thanks. Show him how giving becomes an act of thanksgiving. Create cards of appreciation for teachers at school and church. Devote family time to a community event. Help your cowboy share his toys as a way to show gratitude for friends.

And never miss an opportunity to remind your boy why you're grateful for him. A grateful heart expands to receive more joy and love—and to give more in return.

Dear Lord, God in heaven, from my bedroll on the ground—I can't help but see Your majesty in the stars sparkling all around. Your Good Book says You have a name for every star I see above, I know You're looking at me too, for I can feel Your love.

FROM "THE COWBOY PRAYER"

THE BAREFOOT BOY
Blessings on thee, little man,
Barefoot boy, with cheek of tan!
With thy turned-up pantaloons,
And thy merry whistled tunes;
With thy red lip, redder still
Kissed by strawberries on the hill;
With the sunshine on thy face,
Through thy torn brim's jaunty grace;
From my heart I give thee joy,—
I was once a barefoot boy!

JOHN GREENLEAF WHITTIER

A Growing Cowboy Is
Loyal

The loyalty of a little boy's heart is priceless! They love unconditionally, and they express their devotion with hugs, kisses, and a sweet "I love you" just when you need it most. Their attachments to siblings, parents, grandparents, friends, God, teachers, and pets are tender but strong. The key to raising a boy into a man of honor and commitment is to preserve that combination of tenderness and strength when your little one connects his heart to that of another.

Cowboys depended on the loyalty of those around them—from their horse to their crew. When everyone watched out for one another, the job went smoothly and safely. Your boy's loyalty expands as those around him extend loyalty…as they watch out for him and make the job of growing up smooth and safe.

Loyalty is a feature in a boy's character that inspires boundless hope.

SIR ROBERT BADEN-POWELL

THE BOY AND THE FLAG
I want my boy to be the best,
I want him to be great;
I want him in Life's distant West,
Prepared for any fate.
I want him to be simple, too
Though clever, ne'er to brag,
But, Oh! I want him, through and through,
To love his country's flag.

EDGAR GUEST

A loyal friend laughs at your jokes when they're not so good,
and sympathizes with your problems when they're not so bad.

ARNOLD H. GLASGOW

A Growing Cowboy Is
A Friend

To a young boy, the importance of having a great friend matches the significance and necessity of a cowboy having a great horse. It isn't something you rush into. There are important matters at stake. The friend or horse must be easy to get along with, loyal, supportive, and good company for the journey.

There are times when your cowpoke will test the waters to see if a classmate or neighbor might be the kind of fella he could play games with, talk to, invite over on a rainy Saturday, or who would make a great partner when exploring the terrain of the playground. If he ever worries that he doesn't have a best friend at recess, just remind him that while he's looking for someone to share part of his journey with, he can work on all the traits that make *him* a good friend. Lead him through these important characteristics of a cowboy and he'll be well on his way to becoming and finding a great friend.

You got to sorter give and take in this old world. We can get mighty rich, but if we haven't got any friends, we will find we are poorer than anybody.

WILL ROGERS

A friend is one of the nicest things you can have, and one of the best things you can be.

DOUGLAS PAGELS

What is a friend? I will tell you. It is a person with whom you dare to be yourself.

FRANK CRANE

Ask a boy how strong he is and he's quick to flex his muscles and make a fierce face. But showing a boy's strength of character is a lifelong process that begins with the years when he's discovering how to be himself and how to follow a path of goodness. Nurture your guy's character with lessons along the way.

Teach him that his actions, good and bad, have consequences and do impact others. Delight in his youthful energy and curiosity. Encourage him to discover his gifts, and show him how using those talents can bring joy to others and fulfillment to his own life. A boy who grows up with a sense of virtue and purpose will become a man of conviction, morals, and meaning.

Character is like a tree and reputation like its shadow. The shadow is what we think of it; the tree is the real thing.
ABRAHAM LINCOLN

How can we expect a harvest of thought who have not had a seed-time of character?
HENRY DAVID THOREAU

Character is a by-product; it is produced in the great manufacture of daily duty.
WOODROW WILSON

Where children are, there is the golden age.
NOVALIS

(31)

I remember seeing a picture of an old man
addressing a small boy. "How old are you?"

"Well, if you go by what Mama says, I'm five.
But if you go by the fun I've had, I'm almost a hundred."

WILLIAM LYONS PHELPS

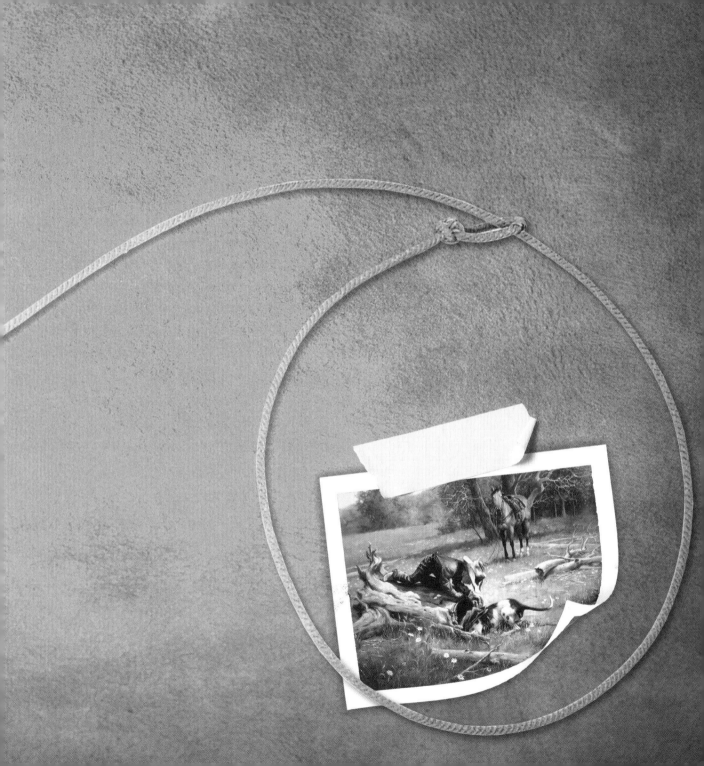